Never Knew Love Like This Before

Pastor D. L. Williams

Table of Contents

Forward by Dr. Michael E. Jackson

Dedication

Preface

Chapter 1: I Wanna Know What Love Is ………… 9

Chapter 2: The Greatest Love of All ………………..19

Chapter 3: So Amazing ….………………………..….32

Chapter 4: I'll Always Love You……………………45

Chapter 5: Let Your Love Flow………………..…..55

Chapter 6: Then Came You …………………….....65

Chapter 7: Reach Out: I'll Be There………………..82

Chapter 8: That's the Way Love Goes……………..94

Final thought

Forward

Pastor D.L. Williams grew up in Aimwell Missionary Baptist Church in Mobile, Alabama. I had the privilege of not only being his pastor, but I pastored his mother, grandmother, great grandmother, brother, aunts, and one of his uncles; the late Bishop Lester Lorenzo Williams. I am not surprised that he has written such a powerful book about love. He grew up in a loving home and family.

In Pastor Williams' book, *Never Knew God's Love Like This Before,* he gives a clear understanding of what love is from seven different religious point of views. He says, "Love is a universal language; a requirement of faith; and the only true source of eternal happiness". The reader is given a healthy introduction to the love of God. Pastor Williams believes that all human creation can obtain His love, depend on it, dwell in it, and be filled with it. We are told that God's love is great, unchanging, perfect, global, available, and giving. We can not earn it, we do not deserve it—God just gives it to us.

This book helps us understand that God loves us even though we are lost, flawed, confused, messed up, and imperfect. God loves us even though we were unlovable. He loved us so much that He gave us his only begotten son; and this son loved us so much that he gave us his life for us. This book challenges the reader to respond such a love by loving God back, in addition to loving others (our neighbors) as we love ourselves, and even our enemies.

Pastor Williams concludes his book by encouraging the reader to commit to the best interest of God and others, as we practice looking after the best interest of ourselves. God called us to love the way he loves. He called us to love people—not naturally, but spiritually.

If you are not a person of faith, this book will lead you to become one. If you are a Christian, this book is a must read! If you consider yourself a child of God or whatever your faith may be, you will be blessed by reading this. The truth is, I could not put it down. I must, and I will read it again.

~Dr. Michael E. Jackson

Dedication

I would like to dedicate this book to a few very important women in my life who all gave me nurturing experiences with love. To my Great Grandmother, Mimie Harris. I love you with all my soul. Thank you for showing me how to love family. To my Grandmother, Viola Williams. I love you dearly. Thank you for showing me how to love God. To my Mother, Sheila Williams. I love you with everything I am. Thank you for showing me how to love myself. Last, but certainly not least, to my lovely wife, Precious Williams. I love you with my entire life until death alone parts us. Thank you for helping me learn how to love others with the agape love of Christ. It is because of you all that I am what I am today.

Preface

Have you ever been in love before? Do you remember the first time you fell in love with someone? That thought alone should make you smile inside and create a warm—if not butterfly—feeling in your heart. Though that memory may be far in the distance of your mind, or maybe a present reality for you, recalling the times you have shared love and experienced it with another, or reveling in the real-time love you share with someone in the present moment makes you feel good inside because love is such a beautiful experience.

Love, in its rawest and purest form, softens and transforms the human heart, and it makes touching such a part of ourselves, which we don't readily get to touch, possible. It helps us to reach a sacred layer of ourselves that normal everyday co-existence with another is powerless to offer. I'm talking about that compassionate, gentle, sympathetic and even sometimes childlike aspect of ourselves that love alone can unearth.

When you truly come to know it in its most sacred form, love is the driving force of your very existence on the earth. All that you do, say, don't do, don't say, experience, and fail to experience is heavily influenced by love or the absence of it.

Believe it or not, love is the very foundation of our human existence, so much so that all religions promote it. Even though you can find many small and major doctrinal differences practiced in the primary religions in remote regions of the earth, the one common thread they have that connects the tapestry of them all is the principal idea of love. This very fact helps us to draw an obvious yet profound conclusion: *Love is vitally important to our co-existence on the earth.*

Let's take a closer look at some examples of how this common thread seamlessly flows through nearly all the major religions of the world, unifying their views on this simple basic principle of love. The main religions of the world fall into two categories: Abrahamic and Indian. These are some of the beliefs a few religions from both categories espouse regarding the principal idea of love:

Abrahamic Religions

Bahá'í Faith

- God created humans due to His love for them; therefore, humans should love God in return.
- Love is the greatest power in existence and the true source of eternal happiness.
- Love is a part of God's essence, and His love for creatures gives them their material existence, divine grace, and eternal life.
- True love for other humans occur when people see the beauty of God in other individual souls.
- Bahá'i adherents should love all humans regardless of religion, race, or community, including their enemies.

Judaism

- Love is an essential ingredient to life.
- The central commandment of the Torah says to love your neighbor as yourself, which encourages individuals to treat each other as equals.
- Love all people, including your enemies.
- Love involves giving without expectation of reciprocity.

- Justice refers to the institutionalization of love within the society.

Islam

- God is so loving He instilled His attribute of love as a basic instinct in humanity, making it man's duty to love each other as God loves us.

Christianity

- The greatest commandment says to love God with all our heart, mind, soul and strength; the second greatest commandment tells us to love our neighbor as we love yourselves.
- We are commanded to love our enemies.
- *Agape* is the highest form of love. It is love that is altruistic and unconditional.
- First Corinthians 13:4-8 says, "Love is patient, kind, does not envy or boast, is not proud, rude, self-seeking, or easily angered. It keeps no record of wrongdoing, does not rejoice in evil. It always rejoices in truth, it

always protects, trust, hopes, perseveres. Love never fails." These verses indicate the principal emphasis is on love.

- Because of God's love for humanity, He sent His Son as a sacrifice to redeem mankind from sin, hell, and condemnation through faith in Him.

Indian Religions

Buddhism

- *Karuna love* is compassion and mercy, which reduces the suffering of others, and it is necessary for enlightenment.
- *Advesa love* is benevolent love. This love is unconditional and requires considerable self-acceptance.
- *Bodhisattva love* involves complete rejection of oneself in order to take on the burden of a suffering world.

Hinduism

- *Prema love* refers to elevated love. One gives up selfishness in love, not expecting anything in return. It also believes "God is love."

Sikhism

- Love is one of the five virtues of life. Love centers around loving the Lord and His creation.
- When one's mind is full of love, the person will overlook deficiencies in others and accept them wholeheartedly as products of God.
- All believers are encouraged to take on godlike virtues, love being the most god-like feature of them all. This act makes forgiveness uncomplicated for the human heart, hate for another impossible, and living in His will attainable.
- Only those who have love will attain God.

As you can see, in seven of the most popular religions around the world, love is a universal language. It is an all-encompassing principle taught in every corner of the earth in every language under the sun. All religions view it as the most essential element among mankind and even all of creation. Love is *the* principal virtue, and our world would be a much better place if we all actually practiced it! Regarding all the tenets of our faith, if we mastered none of them except love, we would be more advanced in our faith and as the human race than we ever have previously.

The problem is that some of us either don't fully understand love, seek to grow in our capacity of love, haven't really experienced real love, or hold a secular worldview of love, which is incorrect because love is a distinctive characteristic of God. How can you adopt a worldly view of a concept that is actually divine? It would seem logical to seek a divine viewpoint of the divine, to see it *not* through the lens of the world but rather through the lens of God. Love is a virtue of God. Yet, as simple as it is, as beneficial as it is, and as powerful as it is, love is the most misunderstood, unlearned, unpursued virtue of all.

Combining some of the aforementioned core ideas about love from these various faiths, we must all agree that love, the most god-like, instinctive virtue given to humanity, is a requirement of faith. *It is the greatest power in existence, and the only true source of eternal happiness. As the most essential ingredient of life, love is perfected when we reject ourselves in order to unconditionally share it with God, all of creation, and all human beings despite their race, religion, or community, as well as with one's enemies, because showing love to this magnitude is the only way to actually know God.*

With this comprehensive understanding of love in full view, it's extremely necessary to call attention to this virtue so that we can actually know it, grow in it, and find the peace, joy, and eternal happiness that come along with it. In order to do this, we must start with the very source of love—*God*. So, with this book, my desire is to reveal God's love for us, explain the essence of human love, and show how—whether the results are good or bad—it is vital to every single relationship we have. They all should be characterized by love.

CHAPTER 1

I Wanna Know What Love Is

And so we know and rely on the love God has for us. God is love. Whoever lives in love lives in God, and God in them.

(1 John 4:16)

In 2012 New York was hit by a historic superstorm named Hurricane Sandy, which reached maximum wind speeds of over two hundred and thirty miles per hour. This event was an unprecedented event for New York at the time because historically, it had not been hit by such a storm in centuries. When Sandy hit, it wreaked devastating upheaval to the area for three straight days, causing millions of dollars' worth of damage.

Immediately after Sandy had finally moved through the cities, leaving hardly any time for the streets to dry, a winter storm followed in its path just days later, causing additional damage to the state. Never before in the history of this country had New York been hit by two historic storms back to back. They were struck by a historic hurricane at the end of the summer storm season, only to be hit again by a epic storm at the beginning of the winter storm season!

This meteorological occurrence was so bizarre and strange that soon after the winter storm hit, the *New York Post* printed a front-page story, entitled "God Hates Us." The writer of the article wondered if the recent unprecedented crippling storms were some sort of divine sign that God was somehow angry or displeased with New York.

This kind of speculation reminds me of one night when I was pastoring in Illinois around the year 2010. I was attending a community event at a hotel but preparing to leave. I met a young white girl crying her eyes out in the lobby, and out of concern, I asked her what was wrong and if she was okay. She looked at me, her face red from crying uncontrollably, and said, "God doesn't love me!" My immediate response was, "Yes, He does," to which she responded, "No, He doesn't!" I asked her why she thought God didn't love her. She began telling me about the break-up between her and her boyfriend, which caused her so much emotional pain that her theological interpretation of her relationship crisis was simply, "God doesn't love me!"

I'm not sure why, but for some reason when things go wrong in our lives, we have a tendency to think God must feel differently about us. This was true of the Israelites, as recorded in the Book of Deuteronomy. Verse

27 of chapter 1 says that as they were struggling in the wilderness, everybody was murmuring that they were in this uncomfortable situation because God hated them, which only revealed that they had a really distorted view of God's love. This warped viewpoint shaped the way they believed, as well as the decisions they made going forward.

This is the problem many believers wrestle with today. Countless believers and non-believers alike are unfamiliar with the nature of God's love. Without a proper understanding of the richness of His love, their distorted perception of His love negatively influences the way they believe, and subsequently, the decisions they make. The truth is, if we all really understood God's love, our lives wouldn't be as confused, our hearts wouldn't be as troubled, and our world wouldn't be as chaotic as it is today.

The number-one problem with the world today is this: *Human creation, as a whole, has a distorted view of God's love.* Some of us know *about* His love, but we don't actually *know* His love. John writes in First John 4:16, "We know, and rely on the love God has for us. God is love. Whoever lives in love, lives in God; and God in them." John shares four things with us in this verse about God's love:

1. We can *know* God's love.

2. We can *rely on* God's love.

3. We can *live in* God's love.

4. We can *be filled with* God's love.

All of these truths about God's love are possible for us to attain. We can be acquainted with it, depend on it, dwell in it, and be filled with it. However, before we can be filled with His love, before we can ever live in His love, before we can even rely on His love, we must first know God's love.

Yet, there's so much to grasp that we will never fully understand His love during the short amount of time we are living here on the earth. Even if God gave us two lifetimes, we could never completely know His love because it is too complicated for us to fully comprehend. We're too human to make sense out of divine love. To be honest, the best we can do is explore it and get deeper *into it*. But even though we can't fully know the full extent of God's love, we can become more intimate with it.

The first aspect we should realize about God's love is that it's great. This means that His love is abundant. God is the Mansa Musa of love. Mansa Musa, a black African king, still holds the world's record as the richest man to have ever lived in the entire world, with an estimated net worth of over four hundred billion dollars. Just like Mansa Musa, nobody ever has or ever will possess more love than God, who has an infinite supply.

Love is the only attribute that ultimately defines God and is His chief glory. In fact, love is the only quality He was willing to die for in order to demonstrate it to the world. When God decided to show Moses His glory, He told Moses as He was passing by that He's a God who's merciful and gracious, slow to anger, and *abounding in steadfast love.*

God was letting Moses know that it was impossible for Him to never have more than enough love. As long as He's God, in every situation and for every individual, He will always have an abundance of love. We need to know this about God's love: God always has more than enough love available for us. He never runs out of love or has just enough love to get by in regard to loving us.

Now, sometimes it is difficult to love certain people because they require so much love. When we aren't rooted deep enough in God, we just don't have the right amount of love it takes to be in relationships with certain individuals.

Some of us right now have family members with whom we can only have a blood relationship because those particular individuals require more love than we emotionally have to give for the relationship to be anything more than that. However, with God, no matter who you are, how you are, or how you think you are, you are never so much the way you are that God doesn't have enough love to give you. He always has an abundance of love available for His creation. His love is, always has been, and always will be—great.

Not only is God's love great, but it's also unchanging. This is the one feature about God's love we misunderstand the most. Sometimes we naturally assume God's love works in the same way we allow our love to work. We don't realize that we are mostly surrounded and influenced by the way the world loves. When we love the way sinners love, we can love somebody one month and despise them the next. The same person we once couldn't see ourselves being without suddenly turns into the one person we hate being around at all. Best friends become worst enemies when the relationship is governed by the world's model of love. With sinners, it's always a thin line between love and hate.

Since we are most familiar with this pattern of love, we wrongly assume that God must be like us, believing He loves us more during certain moments but less in others.

This is not, however, the nature of God's love. God's love is perfect and thus never changes. As long as we are alive on the earth, God will never love us any more or less than He does right now. He loves us not only with a great love but also with an unchanging love. His love doesn't decrease when we're wrong or increase when we're right. His love for us just is! It is always available in its most perfect form without reservation or limitations.

The reason this is true is due to the fact that God's love doesn't depend on us. His love is never consistent with who we are or fail to be. Instead, His love exclusively depends on Himself. It's never based on our actions or inaction but on His divine character alone. Who or how we are has no bearing on God's love. His love is specifically based upon who He is, not on who we are.

As long as God is God, His love will always be perfect. God will always be consistent in His thoughts towards us. His love for us will forever be irrevocable, which is a legal term that means "unable to be pulled back or retracted; to be beyond recall; to be changeless." So regardless of how much our morals, values, actions and in-action in life may change, God's love will always remain consistent. He is the same yesterday, today and forevermore, and the same is true of His love. It never changes.

But not only is His love unchanging; it's also never-ending. Remember when God revealed Himself to Moses in the Book of Exodus? He told Moses that He was a God full of grace and mercy, a God who was slow to anger and abounded in *steadfast* love. That word "steadfast" means to be "everlasting." It means to go on and on for a long time, uninterrupted. This means as long as you are alive, God will never stop loving you because His love stands forever.

Even when God gets angry with us, He will still love us. In Isaiah 54:8, God says, "In overflowing wrath, for a moment I hid my face from you; but with everlasting love I will have compassion on you," which means that even when He is upset with us, He still loves us. Even when God has to punish us for our sins, He still loves us. Hebrews 12:6 says, "God chastises those He loves." Just because God has to deal with us from time to time doesn't mean He doesn't love us or has stopped loving us. Jeremiah 31:3 says, "I have loved you with an everlasting love." This is the kind of love God has for us—a love that never ends.

When you said your first curse word, God still loved you. When you told your first lie, He still loved you. When you sold crack in your neighborhood, when you were sitting in prison serving time, every time you had sex when you weren't married, when you backslid into sin and got caught up with "certain entanglements," as Jada Pinkett famously prefers to call it, God still loved you. He still loved you and still loves you now because He loves you with an everlasting love.

What you need to know about God's love for you is that this love is currently available to you by faith. All you have to do to receive it is just believe God loves you like this, and then you just live your life like a person who knows God loves him/her abundantly with a never-ending, unchanging love. Other than this, you don't have to do anything more to be loved by God because He already loves you. You just have to receive it by faith.

God's love isn't earned or deserved. It's only man's love that requires you to be worthy or deserving. However, you can't work for God's love because His love isn't set up like that. Before you ever became a living human being, God already loved you enough to make sacrifices for your good.

Even while we were sinners and didn't even know enough about God to even desire His love, He loved us. So there's nothing more for us to do for this love from God but just believe that this is the kind of love God has reserved just for us—a great, unchanging, never-ending love.

CHAPTER 2

The Greatest Love of All

"God so loved the world that he gave his only begotten Son that whosoever believes in him shall not perish but have everlasting life."

(John 3:16)

One of the greatest tragedies about our faith is that many of God's children are largely unfamiliar with His love for us. Many of us claim to have this religious conviction called Christianity, yet we are largely unaware of just how much our Father truly loves us.

The truth is that we have thrown the statement "God loves you" around so loosely that it seems to have lost its true value within the faith. "God loves you" has become such a religious idiom that most of us have never found it important enough to learn more about it. We just take this phrase at surface value without any real desire to actually discover what all is involved with it.

God's love has become so commonplace that it doesn't even fascinate the average Christian like it really should. We think we already understand it because we are so familiar with the love of man, failing to realize that man's love for man pales in the face of God's love for man. This is a revelation that we can only receive once we become students of God's love.

As stated previously, this journey doesn't start with knowing *about* God's love but with *knowing* His love. There's a specific difference between the two terms. When you know *about* something, all you have is certain *information*; but when you *know* something, you either have a certain level of personal *experience with it* or personal *intimacy with it.* Regarding God's love, more people know *about* it than those who actually *know it.* The problem with this situation is that what you only know *about* isn't life changing. It's only what you *know* that changes your life.

This is the reason Paul prayed in Ephesians 3:18 that believers would all be able to fully comprehend the height, depth, length and width of God's love—that Christians everywhere might one day understand the full measurement, the complete dimension, the entire extent, the total capacity, and absolute magnitude of His love. And what better way to do that than by turning to one of the most well-known Scriptures that refers to His love for us?

"For God so loved the world that he gave his only begotten son that whomsoever believes in him shall not perish, but have everlasting life."

(John 3:16)

One theologian calls this verse the greatest statement ever written in the Bible because everything about it is the greatest.

God—the greatest lover
So loved—the greatest degree of love
The world—the greatest congregation
That he gave—the greatest act
His only begotten son—the greatest gift
That whosoever—the greatest opportunity
Believes—the greatest simplicity
In him—the greatest attraction
Should not perish—the greatest promise
But—the greatest difference
Have—the greatest certainty
Everlasting life—the greatest incentive

But not only that, John 3:16 challenges ideas and concepts created by the world that come along to hinder our efforts to know His love. The opening phrase, "For God," confronts atheism by debating the claim that there is no God. However, God is mentioned here because He's real, and not only is He real, but He is also the reason for all the love we have available to us today.

The second phrase, "so loved," challenges the idea that God is an impersonal force, meaning that He is just divine energy, thus incapable of having a personal relationship with people, and He has no emotions, which makes Him incapable of "loving us." But according to this text, God not only loves us, He also loves us with an unlimited degree of love. He *so* loves us!

"The world" speaks to nationalism, the ideology that God only loves certain kinds of people. But this verse's claim is that God loves *everybody* in the world.

"That he gave . . . so that whosoever" deals with psychological egoism, a theory that suggests all behaviors are motivated by self-interest and anything God does, He ultimately does it for Himself. However, John's revelation from God through the words of Jesus is that what He did wasn't for Himself but absolutely for "whosoever."

"His only begotten son" confronts the Islamic doctrine that aggressively denies the sonship of Jesus. The Quran consistently rejects the idea of a begotten son of

God. However, the Christian faith teaches that God not only has one begotten Son, but that He also gave Him as a sacrifice for the world.

"So that whosoever" takes issue with exclusivity, the idea that Jesus only died for certain people. Yet His death was not a display of exclusivity but rather one of great inclusivity. God didn't leave *anybody* out. There are no exceptions to those who benefit from His love. The love God demonstrated by the sacrifice of Jesus Christ on Calvary was for *everybody*.

"Believes in him" challenges the idea that faith is an illusion and a virus of the mind. According to John, having faith is a spiritual prerequisite for attaining our eternal hope. This scriptural mandate requires us to believe in Him because our faith produces eternal rewards for us.

"Perish . . . everlasting life" challenges the theory of annihilation, which says there is no heaven or hell—when we die, we just die! Annihilation says there is no such thing as a final judgment or an afterlife. But according to John 3:16, perishing and everlasting life involve two real destinations after this life is over. The Bible says we all will give an account for every deed done in the body, along with every word spoken from our mouths. Our faith teaches that we all will be judged, and that judgment will either land us in heaven or hell.

"Shall have" challenges skepticism. These two words alone guarantee God's promise of eternal life. There is no need to doubt or be skeptical about our eternal reward. The words, "shall have," give us the assurance that God's promises to us are real.

John 3:16 is the greatest statement in the Bible about God's love for addressing and challenging ideas that come along to discourage our faith in His love for us. But not only that, this verse also reveals other things about God's love for us: It shows us that God's love is global. Every individual in the world represents the object of God's affection. He so loved *the world.*

And when God loved it, it wasn't a righteous world but a messed-up one. Yet, even in its most decayed form, God still loved it to an immeasurable extent, which shows us that His love is able to love even the unlovable. Whether people agree with it or not, God loves everybody in the world. He loves alcoholics, porn stars, people with mental illnesses, high-school drop-outs, street gangsters, people who have been failures at life, children with behavioral problems, racists, prejudiced people, those struggling with addictions, tax frauds, looters—you name it! He loves deadbeat daddies, the woman with more baby daddies than she has babies, the husband who's having an affair, the wife who's been cheating on her husband for the past two years, the neighbor who refuses to speak, the person who's on trial right now for taking another person's life, etc.

I know some of us may not agree with all of these examples of people in the world being loved, but whether we agree with it or not, God's love is global, and there is nothing we can do about it. He loves everybody. He loves Baptists, Catholics, atheists, black people, Asian people, Americans, Middle Easterners, and Europeans the same. He loves gay people, straight people, free people, imprisoned people, people with money, people on governmental assistance, children born to married people, and children born in sin. God so loves *everybody* because His love is global.

God's love is also giving. You see, love is not love without something that's been given. If you say you love somebody, but you've never given them anything, then what you have for that person isn't love at all because love gives. It gives from a place of abundance, and most importantly, it gives from a place of sacrifice. John 3:16 tells us that God loves us so much that He gave us something. From a place of sacrifice, He gave us His only begotten Son, Jesus *the Christ.*

In the Hebrew language, the word for *love* is *ahavah*, which means "to give." Interchangeably, it can either mean "I give" or "I love." This makes love more than just a feeling, but rather an action word that indicates giving accompanies love. Giving is a condition that creates, demonstrates, and sustains love. Without giving, there can be no true love connection.

Meaningful and loving relationships are only created and sustained when they are accompanied by mutual giving. If you don't give some of yourself, including your time, honor, respect, possessions, wisdom, or emotions, then you don't love these persons like you may say or think you do, because love is always accompanied by giving.

But don't misunderstand this. Everybody who gives you something doesn't necessarily love you. It's possible to give without loving, but it's impossible to love without giving. Never forget this principle. This is why the Devil shouldn't be able to cast a doubt in your mind about God's love for you. The Bible makes it clear that God loves us *so* that He *gave* something for us. This is the divine nature of love—love gives. Even when you don't deserve it, love gives.

That's why bad children tend to have good Christmases. Despite how bad and hard-headed they may be, their mothers, fathers, or grandparents still love them. Even though they failed math and maybe are struggling in science, somebody loves them. Although they've been in detention and suspended from school, somebody loves them. In spite of themselves, somebody in their life still gives to them, because they are still loved. Indeed, love gives.

Not only does John 3:16 display the global and giving nature of God's love, it also shows how generic His love is. The key term in the Scripture suggesting this concept is the term, "whosoever." When a product is "generic," that means it has no specific application and is not limited to a certain group. This perfectly describes the open availability of God's love. His love isn't confined by specialization. It isn't reserved for a special group of people. You don't have to speak in tongues for God to love you. You don't have be baptized first, know the Scriptures by heart, or dress a certain way. No, His love is *generally* available to us just as we are.

Every "whosoever" alive in the world is already qualified and approved to be loved by God. In fact, you don't have to be a Christian for God to love you. God already loved you before you ever found out what "religion" meant. He loved you before Jesus even came to the earth in human form to die for your sins. God loved you before Christianity even became Christianity.

Remember, God so loved the world that He gave His only begotten Son. His love is what prompted Him to give you Jesus, proving that He loved you before Christianity was even a reality on the earth. Indeed, having religion or faith doesn't even qualify you for God's love. God loved you before you knew enough about Him to believe. Your birth on this earth is what qualified you.

Faith, however, qualifies you for God's *eternal* love. Even though you don't have to be a Christian to receive God's love in your time, you must have faith in Jesus Christ to receive God's love eternally. Earthly time is just temporary. The unconditional love that we all are receiving from God right now is only fit for this timespan. God will always love us as long as we exist within the interim of time. But when we die, if we failed to love God in return by having faith in Jesus, this brief life on earth will have been the only time we've experienced God's love. We would never know what it means to be loved by God eternally. Those without faith do not gain that reward of eternal life, when all of us as believers will bask in the eternal love of God. But if you get saved and believe in Jesus, when your time on the earth is up, you will know His love within a continuum that greatly transcends time. You will experience His love in and for eternity.

That's one benefit of being saved. Salvation secures God's eternal love for your soul when your life is over. You don't have to do or believe *anything* to be loved by God in earthly time. Yet, those decisions you make during your time on earth will determine if you'll experience the eternal love of God, which is a completely different kind of love than what you receive in finite time. This is the love you and I should be using our time to attain—the eternal love of God. This everlasting dimension of His love He only reserves for those who have faith in Him and do His will.

Also, according to the Bible, God's eternal love isn't just available for certain people in the world. It's available for *whosoever*. Whether you secure it for yourself or not, everyone in the world is a "whosoever," so the eternal love of God is available for us all by faith.

Every drunk on the street is a "whosoever." Every predator in prison, along with every man, woman, and child in the world who doesn't own a Bible today, is a "whosoever." Regardless of our present state, regardless of what we've done or how we've done it, every one of us can turn our lives over to Jesus, and, as a result, not perish but have everlasting life and secure the eternal love of God for our souls.

Don't let the enemy of your soul or anyone in this world tell you that you're too messed up to be saved. You are a whosoever, and God wants to love you eternally. Don't allow anyone to tell you that because you've made too many embarrassing mistakes with your life, God has no interest in you. You are a whosoever, so God loves you enough to save you. Any human being who acknowledges and follows Christ becomes a new creature in God's eyes. Old things have passed away, and all things will become brand new for you.

No matter who "you" are, God's love is global, giving, and generic. He will save anybody. All you have to do is trust Him and His promises enough to open your heart up to His love—and then accept it.

Believe that He feels about you the way His Word says. Accept His truth and receive His Word by faith. Start today living your life like you know God loves you just the way His Word confirms and reveals He does. Today, accept the fact that you are loved with the greatest love of all, just as Jesus stated in John 15:13, "No greater love has a man than this, that a man lay down his life for his friends."

CHAPTER 3

So Amazing

Now the tax collectors and sinners were all gathering around to hear Jesus. But the Pharisees and the teachers of the law muttered, "This man welcomes sinners and eats with them."

(Luke 15:1-2)

Mike Tyson is inarguably one of the greatest heavy-weight boxing champions of all time. He ferociously dominated the sport for over a decade, knocking most of his opponents out in the first round. At the seasoned age of fifty-three, he decided to re-enter the ring for an eight-round "charity match" with another seasoned fighter, fifty-four-year-old Roy Jones Jr. Known for his tenacious knock-out power and his violent yet fearless approach to the sport, when asked by a reporter if he would try to knock Jones out in the match, Tyson responded, "Hey man, I only know one way to fight, and that is just what it is."

In the last chapter, I told you that God's love was global and He loves everybody. For any "whosoever" that desires to be saved, God loves them enough to save them. You can go to every prison in the world, pull up every single inmate's name who is alive and presently serving time, and read about all of their crimes, and the answer will still be the same—God loves them. You can present to me some of the most notorious criminals in the world who have committed the most heinous crimes, and without hesitation, I'll give you the same exact answer. If they are alive and have breath in their bodies, even though God's anger may possibly still burn against them, His love for them remains because He still loves them enough to share the greatest gift He's ever made available for man: the gift of salvation. No matter how much some may cringe at this, it just is what it is!

What some of us need to grasp is the fact that God loves all of us until no more of us is left to love. God loves us until the very last breath we breathe. If the opportunity is there, a notorious sinner can use his very last breath to sincerely appeal to God's love and salvation with all of his heart, and God will save him. He loves all of us enough to save us, even if He has to save us in the very last moment of our lives.

But when some of us read this, we view it with a worldly heart. The first thing that comes to mind is, "That's not fair." We just don't understand how a person can get saved while taking their last breath and make it to heaven after living an entire life in sin, when others have lived a life of righteousness for years to make it into eternity with God. However, the reason this is possible is simply because of God's love. Due to His love, a person who gets saved on their death bed will receive the same salvation that everybody else gets who has been saved for decades.

This is a kingdom truth that Jesus demonstrates in a parable found in Matthew 20. In that parable, Jesus talks about a man who went out around six o'clock in the morning to hire workers to labor in his field for one day's pay. The first workers he came across at six o'clock that morning agreed to work in his field for one day's pay. He went out again around nine o'clock and found more workers willing to work in his field for one day's pay. He went out a third time around noon and found more workers willing to work in his field for honest pay. Finally, he went out one last time around five o'clock that evening and found more workers willing to come labor in his field for pay that was right. At the end of the workday, around six p.m., the landowner decided to pay everyone, from last hired to first hired. The five p.m. workers got in line and got paid first. The noon-day workers got paid second. The nine a.m. workers got paid next, and then finally the six a.m. workers got their pay.

But when the workers got paid, the commotion began. When they looked at the five p.m. workers' paychecks and compared it with their own, in their minds, their pay wasn't enough. All of them worked different hours, but all of their paychecks were all the same. This didn't go over too well with the six a.m. workers who worked the longest hours. They felt they should have gotten at least more pay than the five p.m. workers who literally only worked the last hour of the day.

But the landowner in the parable replied to the most vocal person of the six a.m. group, "Friend, you haven't been wronged! You all agreed at six o'clock this morning to work for me today for one day's pay, and that's what I paid you: one day's pay. Now, don't worry about everybody else's pay, because don't I have the right to do whatever I want to do with my business and my money? The landowner then asked this convicting question, *"Or are you just angry that I've been good to everybody?"*

Jesus explains that this is how God's kingdom works. All God knows to pay is what He promised—eternal life to whosoever believes in Him and His Son, Jesus the Christ. Who gets saved, how they get saved, or when they get saved is none of our business. Salvation is God's business!

Who are we to get angry because somebody got saved in the last hour of their lives? The only thing we need to concern ourselves with is that He was true to His promises and saved us when He saved us.

If you're worried about anybody else's salvation experience who got saved at the last hour, you may be like the six a.m. workers in the parable. You just may simply be mad because God is so good to everybody, particularly to the people you think don't even deserve it. But regardless who raped who, who shot John, who slept around with Mrs. Mary or who Mrs. Jones had a thing going on with, none of us is any more worthy of God's love than they are because our particular sins aren't theirs.

We all still have sinned and come short of the glory of God. His holiness is too perfect to measure how short our individual "short" is, in contrast to the shortness of the next person. In regard to God, either you're completely in His glory, or you're short. Either way, to God short is just short. There is no "a lot of short" and "a little short." With God it's just *short*. However short of God's glory a person is for sex-trafficking young girls is the same amount of short you are for dishonoring and disrespecting your supervisor at work. How short a person is for paying someone to kill a family member for life insurance money is the same short you are for being a busybody (a person who gossips). You are no more deserving of God's love than they are, just because your sins are different. Sin is sin. Short is just short.

We're all undeserving of His love. Yet, His love is equally available to them just as much as it is to us because we all are "whosoevers" in His sight.

The only people who truly have a problem with this are self-righteous religious types like the people in Luke 15, better known as the Pharisees. This was a group of people who felt as if the love of God was only reserved for those who deserved it—for people who did everything right by the book to get it. In fact, the Pharisees believed they were undeserving of even receiving teaching of the holy principles in God's sacred Word.

This is why they took up such an issue with Jesus, who displayed God's love for questionable people without any bias. In the text, they not only found Jesus teaching God's sacred Word to sinners, but they also noticed that He even had the audacity to eat with them, which was the ultimate prohibition for the Pharisees. In the Jewish culture, you didn't just break bread with anybody. Sharing a meal symbolized closeness and friendship. You didn't just sit down at mealtime with anybody, especially those with questionable character. Yet Jesus was socializing with a group of questionable people—and eating with them. Jesus was clearly sharing God's love with them in a non-judgmental setting and fashion. But even though these undeserving sinners were experiencing the love of Jesus Christ the way they did, the self-righteous, religious people felt Jesus had no business being so loving and friendly with a bunch of sinners To them, He had no business receiving them because they were sinners.

Knowing this was the way they felt deep within their hearts, Jesus decides to tell three short parables to explain and illustrate God's love for sinners in the world. To open everybody's eyes and impart truth to everyone around about God's love for questionable people, Jesus tells parables about a lost coin, a lost sheep, and a lost son. These three parables come together to shed light on a few gospel truths, one being that God loves the lost.

In each one of these parables, somebody lost something. The woman lost a coin, the shepherd lost a sheep, and the father lost a son. As Jesus tells these parables, one common thread He intentionally mentions about them is that each person who lost something acted like they loved what they lost. When the woman lost the coin, she didn't just chalk it up as a loss and move on with the rest of her day. Jesus said she lit a lamp, swept the entire house, and committed herself to such a methodical search that only one thing could make her stop—finding that coin! So much of a commitment to such a thorough search conveys one message: she loved what she lost.

The same is true of the shepherd who lost a sheep. He didn't just say "Oh well," and start tallying up the monetary value of the ninety-nine sheep he had left. Instead, Jesus said he left the ninety-nine in an open field to go looking for the lost one. Like the woman, the shepherd conducted a diligent search in which he committed himself to only one thing that could make him stop: finding that one lost sheep. Luke writes that he went after it *until* he found it, indicating that he loved what he lost!

Now, when the father lost his son to the world, unlike the woman and the shepherd in the first two parables, he didn't go looking for his son. Unlike the sheep and the coin, his son wasn't geographically lost. Wherever his son's location, it was exactly where he wanted to be, making his son just mentally and morally lost. When someone is in this condition, there's nothing anyone can do to find them. Mentally and morally lost people have to do some soul-searching to find themselves, which is what the prodigal son did in verse 17: "He came to himself." This means he finally came to his senses and decided to go back home.

Although the father didn't look for him when he was mentally and morally lost, Jesus tells us when the father saw his son in the distance, he was overcome with compassion and ran out to meet his son. Without talking about why he left, without rubbing his failure in his face, without beating him up with guilt for him wasting his inheritance, the father did something that was staggering. He gave his son the best of everything he could think of to give him. Such actions show that this father loved what he lost.

You may be reading this from a lost place. Somewhere, somehow, like the father in the parable of the prodigal son, God lost you. Maybe He lost you to drugs, the pagan patterns of this world, non-religious beliefs, or even some cultic beliefs, but somewhere He lost you. Yet just because you are lost right now doesn't mean God has less love for you in your lost state of mind. God still loves you even when you're lost.

This is the very epitome of His love. Our Bible teaches us that while we were yet in our sins, lost in the world, Christ died for the ungodly. Romans 5:8 says that through Christ, God demonstrated His love for the lost in that while we were yet sinners, Christ died for us. His actions demonstrate that He loves the lost. God hasn't stopped loving you just because you are lost right now. If you're lost somewhere in jail or prison right now, lost in your faith, or lost in some strong drug addiction, God still loves you. What Jesus did on Calvary proves He loves the lost.

But not only does He love the lost, God also loves the least. When the lady lost her coin, it didn't have much value by itself. She had ten coins but lost one. So technically, the nine coins she had left were more valuable than the one she lost. She could have been satisfied with the collective value of the nine and just accepted the least valued coin as a loss. But even though the value of the one coin she lost wasn't worth enough to even look for it, she showed that regardless of its minimal value to others, it still had great value to her. She cared enough to look for it, even though to others it wasn't worth much.

The shepherd who lost a sheep and left ninety-nine behind to find it knew that one sheep wasn't worth leaving the ninety-nine. A basic mathematical calculation would show him that he had more to lose by leaving the ninety-nine than he had to lose by just leaving the one out there lost. The one sheep had the least value, so it just wasn't worth the risk. Yet, the shepherd left the ninety-nine and went looking for the lost sheep *until* he found it.

What about the prodigal son? Remember, his father gave him his portion of the inheritance, but he spent it all living a fast life in the world. So when he came back, he was broke. When he came back, he wasn't worth anything because he gave his entire net worth to the world. The oldest son still had his inheritance, so his net worth was still intact, which meant that of the two sons, the youngest was worth the least. But when he came back home, his father treated him like he was worth much more. He gave him the best of everything after he returned home, his personal worth being absolutely nothing. Though he had lost all his value in his brother's eyes, he still had plenty in his father's eyes. His father demonstrated that when one of his children wasn't worth much to others, he's still worth everything to him.

This is Jesus' core message: God loves the least of us, even when others are unable to see our value beyond our accomplishments or aside from our failures. So if you are the least in your family—God loves you. If you're the least attractive, accomplished, educated, thought about, or anything else—God still loves you. If you don't feel valued by anybody else, know that you're valued by God, and to

God, you are worth it. Regardless of where you've fallen, or whether you've gone astray and gotten away from your Father, you're still His child. You may be lost and you may be the least, but you're still His.

That woman's coin was lost and it was the least, but it was still her coin. That shepherd's sheep was lost and it was the least, but it was still his sheep. The prodigal son was lost and he wasn't socially worth as much as his brother was when he came back home, but he was still the father's son. Likewise, no matter how lost you are today, or how least you may feel, you need to know that you still belong to God. You're still His son or daughter. You're still His creation, still beautifully and wonderfully made. You are *still His.*

And when you belong to Him, you can end up in the wrong position, but you still have your place in God. The coin fell out of its position, but when the woman found it, she put it back in its place. When the sheep went astray, it was out of position, but when the shepherd found it, he put it back in the fold. When the youngest son left his father's covering and ended up in a pig pen, he was out of position. But when he came back home, his father simply put him back in his rightful place: sonship.

Like these characters in the parables, you may be out of position right now. Maybe you've been out of place for a long time now. Maybe you fell out of place, or maybe you just willingly went astray. However it happened, you allowed the world to take the value your father gave you. But the good news is that even though you've been out of position, God can put you back in place. He'll put you back in His grace, favor, will, and your place of purpose.

CHAPTER 4

I'll Always Love You

See what kind of love the Father has given to us, that we should be called children of God.

(1 John 3:1a)

As we've embarked upon this journey of really understanding the love of God, we have discovered that God's love for us is a great love, it is generically global, and it is available for everybody in the world. We know God's love is never-ending, unchanging, and even reaches the lost and the least. God's love is amazing!

I literally cried one day while truly becoming aware of just how much God really loves us. With honesty regarding myself, I cried about this love I don't even deserve. You see, some people are different than I am in that they actually believe they deserve God's love. But others of us know better. We know ourselves well enough to realize that we aren't anywhere close to worthy of being loved the way God loves us. To be honest, when we consider the love God has for humanity, and the results that His love produces for us, it should naturally create a great deal of admiration and appreciation for that kind of generous love.

The beloved apostle helps us with this consideration in First John 3:1. In this short verse, he doesn't describe God's love for us but simply calls on us to behold it, study it, and be amazed by it. What John calls us to consider with great wonder and gratitude is not only just the reality of God's marvelous love, but also the glorious end to which His love brings us.

He writes, "See what kind of love the Father has given us." The word "kind" in the original language of the text points to the absolute quality of His love. John wants us to take in the excellence of God's love, the superiority of God's love, as well as the unmatched value and great significance of God's love. With the use of this one word "kind," John strategically communicates that God's love is *not* a low-quality or mediocre love but rather a top-quality, exclusive caliber of love. It's a love that cannot be surpassed.

Nobody can outdo the way God loves you. This Scripture tells us that this is the kind of love we have *been given*—not that we've "earned," "worked for," or "deserved." In the Greek, this phrase is in the "perfect indicative" verb form, meaning that it's an action completed in the past and its effects still continue in the present. God gave us this quality love a long time ago, and it still continues to be available for us right now today.

After all the iniquity that has been committed by man, after all the racism, immoralities, injustices, and wars inflicted on this earth that have claimed lives, God's love continues to be available to us. After all the sinful acts we've personally done, after all the shady behavior we've engaged in, after all the words we've spoken that have hurt others, and all the things we've done to degrade ourselves, God's love continues to be available to us.

This is the love that John wants us to behold. He wants us to take our time and notice this great, never-ending, unchanging, global, giving, generic love that God willingly shares with the lost and the least—that love which is just as much available to whosoever today as it was when it was first given.

But not only that, He also wants us to realize the ultimate immediate effect of this unparalleled love: "that we should be called children of God." God gave us the best of His love so that we could become more than just servants but also His sons and daughters through faith. Also, He could be more than just our God but also our Father because there are benefits to having a loving father.

On August 9th, 2020, I got a call at six o'clock in the morning that my daughter had just been involved in a bad car accident and appeared to be badly injured.

I could hear my baby in the background sounding as if she was gasping for air. I immediately got dressed and rushed to the scene to see about my child. I left the house so quickly I don't remember how or when I put my shoes on! My wife didn't even get a chance to make it to the car. By the time she got dressed and made it to the garage, I was already on the highway speeding on two wheels trying to get to my daughter. When I got there at the scene of the accident, I learned that the driver of the car had fallen asleep at the wheel and ran into a truck. Although the other two girls in the car were able to walk away from the accident, my daughter had to be taken to the hospital.

I asked one of her friends who was uninjured if she had called her father. She said to me, "No, I can't call my daddy; he's of no use." I then asked the other young lady if she had called anyone to come pick her up, and she replied, "No, because I don't really have anybody to call who can help us. My daddy ain't even worth talking about." The other young lady who originally called me chimed in again, and said, "Mr. Williams, we only called you because out of all our daddies, we knew that you were the only one actually worth something. We knew that if we called Kay's daddy, you would come help us!"

Soon afterward, they put my baby inside of that ambulance in pain with tears in her eyes. The whole time, she was crying for her daddy! I wanted to get in with her, but because of COVID-19, they wouldn't let me get in the ambulance with her. So I stopped everything and said, "Well, if I can't go, I'm going to at least pray before ya'll take her, because we believe in prayer!" Right there with everybody standing around the ambulance, I prayed! I prayed for my daughter, the ambulance crew, the fire fighters on the scene, the police, the other passengers and the hospital staff on shift that had to receive my baby. I prayed for *everybody* in Jesus' name!

Now, I want you to understand that I didn't do all of this because my daughter is a perfect angel, because she's not. I didn't do it because she has always done the right thing, because she hasn't. I didn't do it because she's never disobeyed me, because she has. I didn't do it because she's never made multiple mistakes or disappointed me, because she's done all of these things and more. But the reason I was so quick to go see about her when she was in trouble was simply because she's my child. Regardless of the bad decisions she may make from time to time, or what kind of situation she may get herself into, I still love her because she's still my daughter. And that's the benefit of having a good father—he will be there whenever his children need him.

When you know the Father loves you, you know He'll come looking for you whenever you call; and not just when you call, but He'll even come when somebody else calls Him on your behalf. Even when you haven't been the best you could be, because you're His child, God will come to your rescue when you need Him. He's a good father who loves all of His children. What He'll do for one of His children, He'll do for all of them because He loves each one of His children the same.

That's the beauty of the parable of the lost sheep. Jesus told about the shepherd leaving the ninety-nine sheep just to find the one in order to demonstrate the depth of God's love for us *on an individual basis.* Leaving the ninety-nine to find the "one" shows just how much God loves us personally. It doesn't matter which one of the hundred sheep ever gets lost, the Good Shepherd loves all of them on a personal level, and would do the same for each of them if they ever became "the one"!

That's why we look foolish, like the oldest brother in the prodigal son parable, whenever we as God's children get jealous of each other's blessings. If nothing else, their blessings demonstrate God's love for His children because that shows what kind of father He is. What He does for one child shows what He's willing to do for all of His children. The old saints sometimes say, *"What He's done for others, He'll do the same for you"* because God's love is personal!

According to John 3:16, He loves us "so," indicating that His love goes to a great extent or an extreme degree. God *so* loved the world that He gave His only begotten Son to die for our mistakes, wrongdoing, and faulty living.

This is why you don't have to chase *perfectionism.* You don't have to be perfect for God to love you! God already loves your imperfect, flawed, confused, and messed-up self. Think about it: If God needed you to be absolutely perfect so that He could love you, He would have *made* you absolutely perfect! But God didn't make you *absolutely perfect* so that He could love you. Instead, He made you *perfect enough.*

You need to get that in your spirit today. You may not be perfect, but you're perfect enough for God's love. You're perfect enough for Him to love you unconditionally. You're perfect enough for Jesus to sacrifice His life for you.

God doesn't need to change you to love you. He already loves you just as you are. But because He loves you, He'll cleanse you and change you for His glory. In Christ, however, you've already been made perfect enough to receive His love. Revelation 1:5 says,

"To Him who loved us and washed us from our sins . . . and has made us kings . . ."

Watch what the text says. First, He loved us, then He washed us, and finally He made us kings (and queens). In other words, because of His *compassion* for us, He *cleansed* us and then He *crowned* us. He loved us while we were dirty and unclean. But because He loved us, He washed us of our uncleanness. This means that anytime we become filthy with sin, the same love that caused God to clean us the first time is the same love that will cause Him to clean us again. No matter how dirty we get because of our sin, God will always love us enough to clean us up. That's why First John 1:9 says, "If we confess our sins to God, he is faithful and just to forgive our sins and clean us up from all unrighteousness."

Don't miss that! Our Father loves us *so*, and He's so faithful with His love that He will clean the filth of any unrighteousness away from us. With any sin by which you have become stained, as long as you are willing to take ownership of it and repent, God loves you enough to forgive you and cleanse you from it. Regarding any unrighteousness you confess to God, He loves you enough to cleanse you and crown you a king/queen again.

I'm talking to a king out there right now who fumbled away his crown. I'm talking to a queen out there right now whose head has been bowed so low in sin that her crown left her head. I'm talking to some kings and queens who have lowered themselves to engaging in so much degrading and unbecoming behavior that they have fooled around and lost their crown.

But I've got some encouraging news for you. If you can just get over your humiliation and shame over dropping your crown long enough to lift your head up again, God will cleanse you and restore your crown. You're still a king /queen even though you just fumbled your crown. If you'll just take ownership of the fact that your head just hasn't been in the right place, *God* will clean you up and crown you again.

I know you've got some regrets right now, but king, if you can just get your head back in the right place, and queen, if you can just find the determination to look up again, God will restore your crown—not because you deserve it, but because He loves you so. And Psalm 136 teaches us that we ought to be thankful for God's everlasting love because everything He does for us is done out of love.

When God woke you up this morning, it was because He loves you. When He allowed you to travel to and from your destination, it was because He loves you. When He gave you something to laugh about that time you were feeling down and out, it was because He loves you. So, everything God does for us is because of His everlasting love for us.

That psalm encourages us to respond to this truth with great gratitude. So, from this moment on, never take God's love for granted. Always be assured of His love for you, and remember to stay thankful for His love towards you, because everything God does for you in this life He does out of *everlasting love.*

.

Chapter 5

Let Your Love Flow

One of the teachers of the law came and heard them debating. Noticing that Jesus had given them a good answer, he asked him, "Of all the commandments, which is the most important?" "The most important one," answered Jesus, "is this: 'Hear, O Israel, the Lord our God, the Lord is one. Love the Lord your God with all your heart and with all your soul and with all your mind and with all your strength.'"

(Mark 12:28-30)

Gary Chapman, the author of *The Five Love Languages,* once said, "Our most basic emotional need is not to fall in love. It's to be genuinely loved by someone who chooses to love you." Although we have already been spending time discovering a small fraction of God's love for us, we must now realize that the love God shares with us is not simply meant for us to receive and selfishly consume. Instead, God has given us His love to be an intricate part of our existence because it plays an important role, both in His will and the overall life we've been given to live. That is, as recipients of the outpouring of God's love, once we recognize how His love flows *to us*, that same love is supposed to freely flow *through us* because His love is designed to be fluid. Once we experience God's love, we are required to express it to everyone in our lives.

But the problem that we are experiencing is that generally we don't seem to be choosing to love others as we should. Many of us are guilty of being "Dead-Sea Christians." We're just like the fifty-three-mile-long lake in Israel that receives its water from the Jordan River but has no outlet for this water, which is one reason it's called the Dead Sea. When water from the Jordan River channels into it, none of that water gets channeled from it anywhere else. Instead, when water from the Jordan River moves into the Dead Sea, it immediately stops flowing and just sits there.

This is what some of you are doing with God's love. Even though you have received the outpouring of His love, it's not flowing out of your life into the lives of other people around you. God's love gracefully flows into your life, but it immediately stops and dies with you. It's not channeling into the lives of others from your heart. Yet that's not how God's love is designed. God's love is supposed to flow *from* your life just as gracefully as it has flowed *into* your life, and it's supposed to be the exact same quality of love you've received from God.

This is another reason some of us are "Dead Sea Christians." When the water from the Jordan River gets into the Dead Sea, the quality of the water changes. The Jordan River's water is life-giving. Thousands of organisms live in and depend on the Jordan River for sustenance. All kinds of fish and plant life can be found in the water. But when that life-giving water mingles with the Dead Sea, the water becomes extremely salty. As a matter of fact, the Dead Sea has such a high concentration of salt, it's known as one of the saltiest bodies of water in the world. It's so salty, nothing is able to live in it. Fish immediately die when they enter the Dead Sea, and no plant life can survive in the Dead Sea either. When life-giving water from the Jordan River flows into it, it becomes completely different. It changes from life-giving to life-ending water.

This is what happens to God's love when it flows into some of our hearts. The quality of God's love changes into something totally different than what you received from Him. When it hits your hard heart, God's love stops being unchanging and becomes conditional. It stops being selfless and starts being selfish. It stops being available for the lost and the least among us and starts being reserved only for the people in your circle.

When the quality of God's love changes in your heart, you become more responsible for hurting, ignoring, and mistreating people than you are for encouraging, inspiring, and building up people. However, the quality of God's love should never change once any of us experience it for ourselves. The way you received God's love is the same way it should flow from your heart. The quality of the love you experienced should be the same quality of love you express.

The first recipient of this life-giving love should not be your intimate partner. It shouldn't flow first to your children, or even to your parents. The recipient of the love that has been given to us by God should first be God. Why? Because you can't successfully love anybody who enters your life momentarily or permanently until you first learn to reflect love back to the one who loved you first.

God would agree with the words of the late great musician Teddy Pendergrass, "It's so good loving somebody, and that somebody loves you back" because this is what God desires from us. What God wants from His children is for us to simply love Him back. But I'm not talking about loving God with our emotions because the love given to us by God is not based on His feelings for us.

When John told us in John 3:16 that God loved us *so*, he wasn't talking about God's feelings for us. Rather, he's referring to God's choice to be committed to us and our best interests in this life. This is what love is: *It's the choice we make to be committed to others and their best interests in life.* This is the real definition for love. Love has nothing to do with your feelings. When God loved us, He didn't love us with His feelings; instead, He loved us with His actions. His actions on Calvary demonstrated that we're His choice, and the only thing He wants in return is for us to simply love Him back.

According to the Scriptures, we can love God in several ways. But Jesus shares with us in the Gospels that the first and foremost way to love God is *"with all our heart, with all our soul, with all our mind, and with all our strength."* From all four dimensions of our human existence, we are commanded not to simply have feelings for God, but to choose to commit to Him and His best interests in this world with *all* of our heart, soul, mind, and strength. Notice if you will that each dimension is associated with the word "all." *God wants a relationship with us in which we are "all in!"*

God has the right to require this of us because when we receive Him into our lives, we don't just get some of

Him but all the richness of His character and fullness of His personality. We get all of His love, grace, goodness, mercy, and favor. Even when Jesus died on Calvary for our sins, He loved us until He had nothing else left to give. He literally loved us to death. He gave all of His life for us, because Jesus was *all* in. This is why loving God effectively requires us also to be "all-in." In the black church, we say, "Ninety-nine and a half won't do!" Though ninety-nine and a half means most, it's still not all-in.

What God requires is for us to be "all in" with Him. He wants us to give Him our all because when He loves us, He loves us with all of Himself. He wants all of our heart, which means we need to be completely passionate about Him. When we love God with all our heart, it means that we are more passionate about Him than we are about anything.

This is how it should be for us as people of faith. We shouldn't be more passionate about money or materialistic things than we are about God. We shouldn't be more passionate about worldly accomplishments and personal achievements than God. God wants to be our number-one priority. That's why the first of the Ten Commandments says to have no other god before Him. He wants our hearts to be "all in" *with Him*—to the point we're more passionate about Him than anything.

But not only that, God also wants us to love Him with all of our mind. This means that we need to support our passion for God with our knowledge of Him. God wants us to know Him. How can you be completely passionate about something that you know completely nothing about? God wants us to understand as much as we can about Him so we can become even more passionate about Him.

This means you've got to read your Bible. Find yourself a translation you can understand and read the Word of God so you can get to know God. If you're new to the faith or new to Bible reading, get *The Message* or the NIV translation. Download it on your phone and read along as your app reads it for you. It doesn't matter how you get it; you just need to find a way to get some of the Word in your mind so you can gain some knowledge of *God*.

Some of you know more about other things than you know about your own heavenly Father. You know every lyric to every hit song on the radio but can't quote one verse in the Bible. At any rate, you shouldn't know more about anything than you know about God. If you do, that's not a good example of loving God with all your mind. You aren't "all-in" with God if you know more about the world than you know about God and His kingdom. God wants us to love Him with all of our minds.

God also wants us to love Him with all our souls. This refers to our individual personalities, which should be a reflection of our love for God. This is why we don't need to just be working on *who* we are but also on *how* we are.

If your personality is nasty, divisive, messy, inconsiderate, or unpleasant, it means you're not loving God with all of your soul. Your personality has too many negative areas that you still haven't turned over to God. You've reserved some of your soul for 'hood-activity and other worldly behavior. But you have to commit all of "how you are" to God so that anytime anyone is around you, regardless of the setting or the situation, they're always getting a soul that's been completely surrendered to God.

That's one of the things that made Jesus who He was. Jesus committed His entire personality to God's best interests. He was the same soul with whomever was around Him, which is why sinners were so drawn to him. Unlike other church folks, Jesus didn't have a nice/nasty soul. He wasn't nice to the people He approved of and then nasty to the people He didn't. He wasn't just nice to like-minded people and nasty to those who thought differently than He did. He wasn't just nice to those of His own race and nasty to people of others. Jesus loved God with His entire soul, which was a reflection of His passion and knowledge of God.

Until you can get your soul consistent with your passion and knowledge of God, you are failing to love Him with *all* of your soul. God wants our entire personality to be consistent with His love. He wants us to commit all of our personality to His best interests.

Finally, Jesus says that God expects us to love Him with all of our strength. This means committing all of our capabilities to the best interests of His kingdom. Anything you are able to do, or capable of doing, should be available to God to be used by Him for His glory.

When the world receives more of the benefit from your abilities than the kingdom does, you're not loving God with all your strength. When you can always be on time for your job but always late for kingdom work, that's not loving God with all of your strength. The same way you're capable of getting up and being on time for everything else in the world is the same way you can get up and be on time for what you've got to do for God. The same way you're capable of putting your energy into other pursuits is the same way you can put your energy into the faith. But when the world is getting the best of your talents and capabilities while God is getting your leftovers, you aren't loving God the way you've been commanded to love Him. You've got to be "all-in" with your strength!

So, God expects the quality of love He's given to us to be reflected back to Him. Our relationship with God is not built on the love we want Him to have, but rather on the love He's already given us. His love is the foundation of our relationship with Him. We can't have a productive relationship with God until we start choosing to be "all-in" with every dimension of our existence (e.g. heart, mind, soul, and strength). This is the most important action we can take as recipients of His love: love Him back with the same quality of love that's been greatly poured out on us.

Chapter 6

Then Came You

One of the teachers of the law came and heard them debating. Noticing that Jesus had given them a good answer, he asked him, "Of all the commandments, which is the most important?" "The most important one," answered Jesus, "is this: 'Hear, O Israel: The Lord our God, the Lord is one. Love the Lord your God with all your heart and with all your soul and with all your mind and with all your strength.' The second is this: 'Love your neighbor as yourself.' There is no commandment greater than these."

(Mark 12:28-31)

"Love experienced should naturally become love expressed."

This is the fundamental idea of the second half of our series: the love God allows to flow to us should effortlessly become the love that flows through us. This principal concept is so vitally important because it's one of the main reasons God has revealed this side of Himself and demonstrated His love to us. Now we can know what love is, what love should produce, and what being loved should feel like to the object of one's love.

Again, love is *not* a feeling. Though many of us like to use the way we feel to gauge the authenticity of our love, this emotional method doesn't properly substantiate love. Love is a choice we make to commit ourselves to an individual's best interests within our material world. Although our feelings can sometimes agree with that choice and commitment, and we are most comfortable about who we love and how we love them when they do, the truth of the matter is sometimes they don't.

Yet, even when our feelings don't align with our commitment to another person's best interests in life, God still holds us accountable for making the decision to stay committed. The reason for this is that love is not built on emotionalism but rather on spiritual obligation. Because of our faith, the quality of love we receive from God must not be contained but conveyed.

Because we receive this love from God first, you and I must make Him the first recipient of the love we return, and we must allow it to flow back to Him. For how dare we love anyone or anything before we return the love first shared with us by God? God is the first entity to love us and make the choice to commit to us and our best interests in the world. As a result, it is only fitting that we at least return that love by choosing to commit ourselves to His best interests in the world, which is spiritually referred to as His will. If you and I desire to demonstrate our love for our Father, we have to be committed to His will!

Jesus taught this in the Gospels when He said in John 14:31, "I do whatever the Father has commanded Me to do so that the world may know I love the Father." Not only did Jesus say this, He also lived it. This is the beauty behind His agonized prayer in the Garden of Gethsemane when He was heavy with anxiety and emotional stress from the thought of taking on the Calvary experience. The Gospels clearly show us that Jesus in His most vulnerable moment, temporarily struggling with His feelings, didn't *feel like* taking on Calvary. However, because He loved God, He didn't allow His feelings to compromise His commitment to God's best interests in the material world. And so, Jesus declared His love for the Father: "Not My will, but Your will be done," confirming that despite how He certainly felt about it, His choice to commit to God's best interests was His priority because regardless of all else, He loved the Father.

So with that same level of commitment, we are called to not only love God but to love Him first. First John 4:19 says we love Him because He first loved us. We've been called to be "all in" with our love by loving Him with all of our heart, mind, soul, and strength. Jesus tells us in this text that this is the greatest commandment. But He goes on further to give us more insight about our responsibility to express the love that we have experienced. Although the teacher of the law who questioned Him in the text only wanted to know the greatest and most important commandment of them all, Jesus takes it upon Himself to provide him with insight into what He Himself calls the second most important commandment of all: "Love your neighbor as you love yourself."

Now, when we look at this second greatest commandment, it's clear that we are supposed to love our neighbor. But that's not our focus here. Instead, we choose to focus on something else Jesus says in this text, which, though it's not commanded, is openly implied: the importance of loving yourself. Again, Jesus states that the second greatest commandment is to love your neighbor *as you love yourself,* a command found a total of nine times in the Old and New Testament indirectly hinting at the importance of self-love. Paul even encourages husbands in Ephesians 5 to love their wives as they love themselves.

Even though this is a subject upon which Jesus never directly teaches and is never a point of focus in the Bible, it remains existentially appropriate for us as Christian human beings to have a healthy sense of self-love. For Jesus to even mention it along with the second greatest commandment means that loving ourselves is equally as important as loving those around us.

Friends, not only should we love God with the quality of love He has loved us, but we also should learn to love ourselves with that very same quality of love. We need to learn how to love *ourselves* the same way God loves us. It's critical that we at least hear this today, because as crazy as it sounds, a lot of people don't love themselves, and therefore need to learn the value of self-love.

First, loving yourself is not a prerequisite or the foundation to loving others. Many people seem to think that when Jesus commands us to love our neighbors as we love ourselves, He is really saying that we can't love others until we first learn to love ourselves. This is a terrible misconception. You don't *have* to master the skill of loving yourself before you can love someone else. Loving yourself is *not* a commandment from Jesus. Instead, He commanded us to love others, which means that whether you love yourself in a way that's healthy and appropriate or not, *not* loving yourself is no excuse for failing to love others.

When Jesus reveals the second greatest commandment of loving others as we love ourselves, He isn't saying love yourself *first*, and then love others. Jesus is rather using comparison language to drive His point home, a teaching method commonly used in the New Testament. A comparison normally sets up a standard or a norm against some other position that's being put forth.

For example, in Matthew 12:13, Jesus healed a man's hand, "making it whole, like the other one." The whole hand was the standard against which the newly healed hand was being measured. In Matthew 17:2, Jesus' face "shone like the sun," making the sun the standard by which the shining of Jesus' face was measured. In Matthew 28:4, the soldiers guarding the tomb of Jesus "became like dead men" when they saw the angel. The appearance of a dead man is the standard by which the stillness of the fearful soldiers were compared against. First Peter 1:24 says that "all flesh is like grass," making the way grass fades the standard by which the fading of man's health, strength, and even life itself is compared.

In all of these Scriptures, a comparison to a standard is made to further emphasize the point that's being communicated. Jesus is using the exact same technique with this command for us to love our neighbors. Jesus doesn't give us two different commands here. He's not commanding us to love our neighbors and love ourselves. He's not comparing a command to a command, but rather He's comparing a command to a standard or norm that's already being followed. People already naturally and normally love themselves. So He's advising us to take that norm and use it as a measurement of how God wants us to love others.

Jesus isn't telling us to love ourselves and then once we learn how to love self, we're ready to love other people. He's saying that in the way you already love yourself, take that same energy and use it to love others.

So loving yourself is not a prerequisite to loving others. Instead, it's the standard we should use in determining how God expects us to love the people around us. Every time we fail to commit ourselves to the best interests of the people around us, we are failing to meet God's standard of love because we are called to love others with the same energy we love ourselves. This is a God-expectation, which you cannot meet on your own. To meet God-expectations, you must have God in your heart.

However, in the words of Jesus, many say, "Lord, Lord" concerning Him, but their hearts are far from Him because their hearts are lacking God. In the words of my great-grandmother Mimie Harris, "Everybody talking about heaven ain't going!" If you don't get God's love in your heart for real, and not for show, you are going to be one of those the Lord tells to depart from Him because He doesn't know you. It goes without saying that a small percentage of us are actually meeting God's expectations. Indeed, a great number of us are nowhere near loving other people the way we love ourselves. This means we've got to be intentional about growing in the love of God.

Not only is loving yourself not a prerequisite to loving others but you must also understand that self-love and self-focus are one and the same. Although Jesus clearly alludes to the importance of loving ourselves, most Christians shy away from the subject because there's an overall negative connotation about the idea of loving oneself in our faith. More often than not, loving oneself is translated as pride and ego. We all know that the Bible teaches how much God hates pride, and how much being ego-driven is frowned upon. Proverbs 8:13 says, "The fear of the LORD is hatred of evil. Pride and arrogance and the way of evil and perverted speech I hate." Galatians 6:3 says, "For if anyone who thinks they are something, when they are nothing, they deceive themselves." Second Timothy 3:2 warns us that stressful times will come in the last days; people will become "lovers of themselves" and lovers of money, full of pride and arrogance. All of these verses are examples of humanity's capacity to turn self-love into something dangerous and destructive.

One danger of self-love is that it may lead us to merely accepting ourselves as we are to the point of suppressing our need for God, and seeing no need for personal change. Whoever and however people are, they just accept it and love it to the point that they feel no need to adjust anything about themselves. Sometimes they may not even see a need to put something as abstract as the concept of a god over themselves in order to exchange the old self for a newer self because they are just fine with their old self. They love the old self just the way it is—physically, emotionally, spiritually, and mentally.

That's a dangerous position because that level of self-love has no need for God, and/or a very limited need for His Word. People like this either have no need for religion, or they pick and choose what limited aspects of the faith they want to incorporate in their lives while they completely ignore other parts.

Churches are full of people like this today. These are the churches that fail to grow, fight at church meetings, can't keep members, always have a mess going on about something, and don't have any real sense of service to God. They love themselves so much that they are picking and choosing which of God's standards they will incorporate into their lives and which they are going to ignore—and that's dangerous.

Another danger about self-love, particularly in today's culture, is that it has become dangerously swallowed up in social acceptance. Self-love can become dangerously nurtured by the wrong source. In a culture dominated by social media, the value of self is becoming attached to social acceptance. The more likes, engagements, and comments you get on your social media posts and pictures, the more you're able to love and value self. But the fewer likes, engagements, and affirming comments you get on your post and pictures, the less you are able to love and value self.

Although this sounds elementary to those of us who grew up in a different era, for this generation it is a very real issue. Young girls are manipulating and mutilating their bodies, trying to look like airbrushed digitally edited photos of strangers they follow on Instagram. Constantly comparing their bodies, stretch marks, and other things about themselves to computerized versions of other people is a trend contributing to increasingly higher rates of depression and suicide for young girls and women between the ages of twelve to twenty-one.

Instead of learning how to love themselves, so many people chase after social affirmation through social media. And when they don't get the nurturing they need from others, they are unable to love themselves the way they should simply because they don't feel socially loved by others or as loved as they see others being loved. So they struggle with accepting themselves because they don't feel accepted by others. But a healthy sense of self-love provides security against shame, low self-esteem, and lack of peer acceptance.

The nature of self-love is to have an introspective prioritization of self that aims towards a deeper level of love and acceptance of self. It is an intentional awareness and appreciation of one's own positive traits that frees us from negative thoughts about ourselves in addition to those other people may have about us.

That's why I can care less about anything negative that anybody has to say or think about me. Even though some people confuse my inability to care with arrogance, it's not arrogance at all. It's just that I've learned how to love myself. The negative thoughts and comments of others about me can't negatively impact my awareness and appreciation of my own positive traits because I love myself. That's what self-love is—the pursuit of your own well-being, as well as the avoidance of shame, discouragement, and insecurity from yourself or others.

Friends, you are expected to love yourself. God has commanded us to love others as we naturally love ourselves. If loving ourselves was wrong, God would not have referenced it as the natural standard of human-to-human love. God has instructed us to use the natural standard of self-love as the benchmark for loving others. How can you meet the commandment to love others when you are failing to meet the standard of loving yourself?

You have to practice loving yourself. If nobody else feels good enough about you to make you worthy of their love, you have to see that you are at least worthy of your own love, because you are. You can search the entire universe for someone more deserving of your love and affection than you, and you will find that such a person doesn't exist. There is no one in all of creation more worthy of your love than you. As much as anybody else in the entire world, you deserve your own love and affection just as much as anyone else whom you choose to give it.

You are literally a once-in-a-lifetime experience, and you don't have very long to experience the best of your own love. You have a finite shelf life. Once you expire, you will never get a chance to experience the quality of your own love again for the rest of time. You will never get an opportunity to know what it's like to be you, or to be loved by you ever again.

You need to love yourself like you understand that this is the way God designed you. He made you inherently lovable and worthy of at least your very own admiration. You should be your own best friend, your own soulmate, your own ride-or-die, your own personal cheerleader, your own encourager. Love yourself!

This may take the form of self-care practices like massages, pedicures, long and relaxing bubble baths, or weekend get-aways. It may take the form of taking care of your body by not eating certain foods or gorging yourself, or compromising your health with food, drugs, sex, and alcohol. It may take the form of simply "being kind to yourself" by taking yourself out on self-dates, stay-cations, buying yourself something you would like, treating yourself to something new, or participating in an enjoyable experience like a concert or an outdoor/indoor activity, reciting positive affirmations to yourself, or meditating on your own strengths and accomplishments to feel good about reaching your goals.

Whatever you do, the idea is to just get you to love yourself because you are inherently lovable. You are supposed to be loved. God loves us so much because He designed us to be loved. This is why it's so important for us to love ourselves.

The idea of us being created with this inherent worth is affirmed throughout the Scriptures. God imparted dignity upon us when He created us in His image in Genesis 1. His image within us is what gives us our inherent value, which exists separately from our appearance, accomplishments, or contribution to society. Psalm 139:14 says we are "fearfully and wonderfully made." God's image in us alone is what makes us wonderful.

No matter how big you are, how much you weigh, how low your GPA was when or if you graduated, how unaccomplished you maybe, how unattractive you are in other people's opinions, how many stretch marks you have on your stomach, how much cellulite is in your legs, how broke you are, what kind of low-paying job you have, or what kind of neighborhood you live in, none of this is a relevant factor for the inherent value God has given you. God made you valuable when He shaped you in His image.

Ephesians 2:10 says that we are God's workmanship. In the Greek language, this means that we are all masterpieces. God paid detailed attention to us when He formed us. Everything about us is intentional. This is how you need to see yourself—as one of God's planned masterpieces. Love yourself as such. The beginning of healthy self-love begins with an accurate view of who we are.

Once you begin here, it then continues with balancing the love we actively have for ourselves and the love we actively have for others. Philippians 2:4 says, "Let each of you look not only to his own interests, but also to the interests of others." In this verse, we see the need to balance the concept of loving ourselves with that of loving others. Without disparaging the principle of looking out for our own best interests in the world, we are encouraged to also look out for the best interests of others. This is the language of love.

Remember, we don't define love as a feeling but as a choice to commit to other people's best interests in life. So when Paul writes for us not to look only to our own interests but also to the interests of others, he is trying to tell us that it's okay to love ourselves, but we must not *just* love ourselves; instead, we have to balance the time we spend loving ourselves with that of loving others. When we just love ourselves without actively loving others, that's not self-love but self-focus. We are then focusing on nobody but ourselves, and self-focus is unchristian and ungodly.

Jesus didn't just focus on Himself, and neither does God the Father. Therefore, we can't fall into the enemy's trap of thinking that we're loving ourselves when we're really just focused on ourselves. We need to practice getting the focus off of ourselves long enough to value and appreciate others. But as we do so, we must balance self-love in a way that honors the divine presence within ourselves and the workmanship that God has invested into making us who we are today.

CHAPTER 7

Reach Out: I'll Be There

On one occasion an expert in the law stood up to test Jesus. "Teacher," he asked, "what must I do to inherit eternal life? "What is written in the Law?" he replied. "How do you read it?" He answered, "'Love the Lord your God with all your heart and with all your soul and with all your strength and with all your mind'; and, 'Love your neighbor as yourself.'" "You have answered correctly," Jesus replied. "Do this and you will live." But he wanted to justify himself, so he asked Jesus, "And who is my neighbor?"

(Luke 10:25-29)

In Luke 10, we find Jesus confronted yet again by a religious lawyer of His time who asks Him two supreme questions of life, which prompts Jesus to share one of the most challenging parables He's ever told. For those of you who are unfamiliar with what a parable is, it is a modern-day story that's usually not true in the form that it's told, but it has some elements of truth within it. Although it's not a true story, it has a host of values and principles that can be gleaned and applied to one's personal life.

Whenever Jesus told a parable, He wanted His

disciples to walk away not only thinking differently, but challenged to live differently as well.

This particular challenging parable told by Jesus was encouraged by two supreme questions:

1. *What must I do to inherit eternal life?*

This is a question that Jesus must have been asked hundreds of times because a great majority of people were consumed with knowing the right things to do in order to gain their eternal reward. And who else would be better to pose this question to than Jesus?

When asked this question, Jesus does the same thing He did for the Jewish scribe in Mark 12 when He asked Jesus for the greatest commandment of all. He points this religious expert to the two greatest commandments of our faith:

a. Love the Lord thy God with all of your heart, soul, and mind.
b. Love your neighbor as you love yourself.

These two commandments come together to emphasize the spiritual obligation we have to express God's love once we recognize how we have experienced it from Him. We must reflect this love—first back to God, and then to those around us.

When considering these two greatest commandments, we must become conscious of the truth that love is vitally important. Love is so powerful that its significance greatly affects the character and lifespan of our entire world. It's so significant that life absent of love is no life at all, but a living hell on earth. Love is the most essential ingredient of life. It is perfected when we reject ourselves in order to unconditionally share it with God and all other human beings despite their race, religion, and/or community.

This is what Jesus is communicating regarding the second greatest commandment He shares with us. We must continue developing the harmony of civilization through our love for others because anything less than loving with this magnitude threatens our present-day society, which is something we are witnessing right now.

All over our nation, chaos and unrest run rampant among the people. The only cure for the chaos we are seeing is for us to redirect our hearts back to loving God and each other. This is what Jesus tells this expert of the law in the text: to please God to the point of securing eternal life, you must love Him as well as your neighbor.

But many people are just like this man in the text. When Jesus responds by giving him the two greatest commandments to secure eternal life, this religious leader reveals himself as the kind of person who feels as if he's already mastered the way to love God. When Jesus gives this brother the two greatest commandments, he has another question only about one of the commandments, but not the other. He makes no inquiry about loving God with all of his heart, mind, strength, and soul, as if to suggest he's already figured that part out. This is a grave mistake many people following God make. They think they already know how to love God and they're already doing a great job at it.

They think because they go to church, they're already doing a good job of loving God. Because they pay their tithes and pray before their meals and bedtime, they're doing a good job of loving God. Because they study the Bible in small groups and have memorized many of the things written in it, they're doing a good job of loving God.

Yet, while they are busy checking all of these boxes to make themselves feel good about being a

Christian, at the same time they're busy being racist, sexist, prejudiced, and discriminatory against other people. While they call themselves serious lovers of God, they are guilty of withholding His love from certain groups of people, and doing so with a distorted sense of justification.

They hate black people, and then they try to justify it with a rational defense. They hate Muslims and try to justify it with logical reasons. They hate white people and try to justify it with historical excuses. They detest gays, lesbians, and transsexuals and have the audacity to attempt to give a good reason for it. They justify it all to a level where they are able to remain comfortable in their faith, while falsely believing that the way they live their lives is a textbook example of loving God.

If this is you, understand that this behavior is deeply contrary to the very faith you profess to follow and live by. Our faith teaches us that people who profess the faith but don't love their brother and sister are not of God. We are taught in our faith that the person who says they love God yet hates his fellow brother/sister is a liar. The Bible's stance is that it's impossible to love God whom you've never seen when you can't even display the capacity to love the brother or sister you are able to see every day.

From this argument alone, we discover that everybody doesn't love God the way He demands to be loved. Loving God is about more than just keeping the religious rituals of the faith. It's also about being able to see the beauty of God in other people's souls, as we look beyond the things that inherently or culturally make us different, and love them.

This is the part about which the religious leader questions Jesus. Presuming he already understood what loving God meant, he questions Jesus further about the commandment to love our neighbor. In his mind, this can't imply *everybody*. To him, everybody couldn't possibly be his neighbor. So he presents Jesus with the second supreme question of life:

2.   *Who is my neighbor?*

"Jesus, You say that I should use the way I love myself as the benchmark to how I should love my neighbor, but who is deserving of such love? Who is worthy of the level of love with which I freely and gracefully love myself?" His question reveals a greater darkness in the heart of man: we have a proclivity to disqualify certain people to be recipients of the same love God has lavished upon us, simply because we don't find them worthy of our expression of God's love, which is a gross misrepresentation of the love of God.

By design, the nature of God's love reaches out for those most undeserving of it. When we turn the love we've received from God that we didn't deserve into something that others must become worthy of, we corrupt God's love by turning it into something that is no longer favorable but fraudulent. Sadly, His version of love then becomes a counterfeit version that expresses itself only to those believed to be worthy, when by design, God's love is best demonstrated when shared with the unworthy.

Our calling is to commit ourselves to the best interests of others at all times, and never to their worst interests at any time. This is one of the many extreme principles of our faith. By design, our Christian ideologies aren't supposed to complement the standards of the world. Instead, they're supposed to exceed them. And the way we exceed the world in regard to loving others is by loving *all* people at *all* times.

But this truth is clearly something this religious leader couldn't believe Jesus was possibly suggesting. So for purposes of clarity, he poses the question to Jesus, "Who is my neighbor?" He specifically wanted to know who the people were that he should love with the same grace by which he loved himself. But Jesus doesn't answer this religious leader's question in the pattern it was asked. Instead, Jesus uses a challenging parable to make this man rethink and redefine his idea of who his neighbor really is. Rather than considering a neighbor as someone deserving to receive one's love, he/she should be viewed as someone who simply shares their love with whomever may need it.

This is the principle of the parable that Jesus reveals in this text. Instead of us constantly trying to identify the worthy people to love, we need to start seeing everybody as worthy of God's great, never-ending, unchanging love.

Jesus' parable makes this principle clear, because in it, He tells of a Jewish man who one day fell among thieves that physically assaulted him, robbed him, and left him for dead. While lying there, unconscious from the attack, a priest and a Levite, two of the most religious people in the Israelite community, encountered him one right after the other.

Although they both saw this brother lying there, Jesus says that they both went out of their way to pass him by. No doubt they both felt justified in doing it, because priests and Levites, according to the Old Testament

Scriptures, were forbidden from coming in contact with a dead body. So knowing this, they both passed this man by, thinking they were loving God. Yet, they failed to show enough compassion and love for their brother to even check on him to see whether or not he was dead or simply unconscious, something they didn't even have to touch him to do.

But the reason they didn't even check on the brother who was down and out was simply because they were liars deficient of God's love. When you have God's love in you, His love won't make excuses and come up with reasons not to commit to another person's best interests. God's love will find a way. And if it can't find one, God's love will *make* a way!

Yet, these two highly influential religious men were deficient of God's love. They looked for a reason not to love this man, and they found one. They rationalized, "We're not supposed to touch a dead body!" They felt disgustingly justified making the decision to just walk away from this brother who, though appearing to be dead, may have still been alive. But they didn't care enough to even check on the man to see if this was an opportunity for them to share God's love. These two men instead became self-focused, only looking to their own interests, something the Bible clearly tells us not to do. Philippians 2:4 says not to look to our own interests only, but also look to the interests of others. Yet these two men failed to be an example of showing this kind of love.

But not everyone in the parable was like this. Someone had to be the hero. Jesus makes someone whom the Jews racially discriminated against and whole-heartedly refused to see as their real neighbor the hero of the story. He makes a Samaritan man the model example of what loving your neighbor looks like. This man had so much of God's love in his heart, and was so aware of God's expectation of him to love all people at all times, that he was compassionate enough to ignore racism and every other cultural divide within his community in the name of expressing God's love to somebody who needed it.

Without considering his race, community, and religion, this Samaritan man values the only issue that matters, which is the one thing they both have in common: their humanity. Without dwelling on their differences, he is moved with compassion by their similarities: they are both human beings created and loved by God. Because he was able to see this despite their differences and the hostile social climate between his race and that of the wounded man, he could still choose to love him. He was able to see someone who needed somebody else to see him and commit to his best interests, which involved saving his life and then helping him heal.

At the end of the parable, Jesus asks the religious man, "Which one of the three men was a neighbor to the man?" Technically, the answer is all of them—the priest, the Levite, and the Samaritan. That's the way God designed it. As part of the human race, we're all neighbors in life.

But just as it is true in the text, so it is within our communities. Even though all of us are indeed neighbors, not all of us are choosing to be neighbors to each other. While a great majority of us are walking by people who need God's love, a very small percentage of us are choosing to be neighbors to others around us because we value them as such.

I believe this is Jesus' resting point. More of us need to choose to be the neighbors God has created us to be, and more of us need to see everybody around us as neighbors of ours. That's what this Samaritan did. This is the life-changing decision Jesus is wanting us to make in our personal lives.

It's always a sad tragedy whenever people are responsible for victimizing others. But such tragedies taking place among us is inevitable because the fruit of evil will always be in season. Yet an even sadder tragedy than this occurs when those of us who claim to know God and serve Him pass by opportunities to love the people around us who desperately need God's love.

This is indeed the greatest tragedy of them all, and it's the only one we have the power to control. We can't stop evil from happening because evil will always be with us. However, we can stop looking for self-justifying reasons to withhold God's love from those among us who need it. And we can only do this when we allow God's love to flow through us without looking for people to be worthy of receiving it. We do this by simply allowing God's love to naturally flow from our hearts to the hearts of those around us who just simply need to be loved.

CHAPTER 8

That's the Way Love Goes

But to you who are listening I say: Love your enemies, do good to those who hate you, bless those who curse you, pray for those who mistreat you. If someone slaps you on one cheek, turn to them the other also. If someone takes your coat, do not withhold your shirt from them. Give to everyone who asks you, and if anyone takes what belongs to you, do not demand it back. Do to others as you would have them do to you.

"If you love those who love you, what credit is that to you? Even sinners love those who love them. And if you do good to those who are good to you, what credit is that to you? Even sinners do that. And if you lend to those from whom you expect repayment, what credit is that to you? Even sinners lend to sinners, expecting to be repaid in full. But love your enemies, do good to them, and lend to them without expecting to get anything back. Then your reward will be great, and you will be children of the Most High, because he is kind to the ungrateful and wicked. Be merciful, just as your Father is merciful.

(Luke 6:27-36)

We have discovered that without a doubt, God loves us! The love with which He loves us is a special kind of love—without conditions, fluctuations, or modification. As long as we live on this earth, whether we recognize it or not, God's love will always encompass us as the crown jewel of His creation.

Our faith teaches that God's love is so transformational, it makes us His sons and daughters, a great distinction that comes with a lot of responsibility. We don't just get to be God's child but then be free of accountability. Instead, being His child is a privilege that comes with a great deal of obligations.

The favorite verse cherished by my now deceased uncle, Bishop Lester L. Williams, was Luke 12:48. Inside of his casket, the Bible lay next to him, opened to the words of Jesus, which have now been engraved on his headstone as well: "To whom much is given, of him shall much be required." As redeemed children of God who were once lost in our sin and bound for eternal damnation but have now been favored to become His children, indeed much is required of us.

One of the requirements of us as God's children is that we reflect His character on the earth. When you receive Jesus Christ into your heart, and receive salvation as the gift of God's love for you, spiritually you become His child and subsequently become accountable for reflecting His character among mankind. As God's spiritual child, some of what's true about Him is now supposed to be true about you, since in some aspect or another, every child reflects the essence of his or her father.

First John 3:9 says, "Whosoever is born of God does not commit sin; because God's seed is in him: and he cannot sin, because he is born of God." According to this Scripture, anyone who is truly born of God cannot continue to comfortably practice sin! When we are truly born of God, a part of His holiness becomes a divine part of us. As a result, the holiness of God, which is a spiritual part of every child of God, will not allow His children to comfortably remain in sin but instead be convicted to repent. When we truly become His children, some of the genetic code of holiness spiritually sequences through us by way of the Holy Spirit, and it helps us to be more like God—who is our Father.

John refers to this as "God's seed" in us. In the original Greek language of the text, John used the word *sperma*, and it's where we get the biological English word, "sperm." In the Greek, *sperma* refers to a life-giving seed. In biology you were taught that sperm is the reproductive cell of life; that sperm is life-giving seed. The reason it is life-giving is because sperm carries DNA.

No, I'm not about to give you a science lesson here, but you do need to know what DNA is in order to fully grasp this principle of God's seed being in us. DNA is a self-replicating material that transports genetic information from one life form to another, which produces certain unchangeable qualities in the new life form that's been created.

Your father is not your biological parent because he signed your birth certificate, or that your mother told you he was your father. It's due to the scientific fact that you share his DNA. Inside of your father's sperm were self-replicating cells that transported some of his genetic information inside of you. Consequently, now there are certain things about your biological father that are genetically a permanent part of you. This means that some of the traits that are characteristic about your father will also be characteristic about you to one extent or another.

For example, if your father dealt with hair loss in his forties and that DNA gene was passed down to you as a male, you can use all the essential oils, shea butter, and creams you want on your hair and scalp, but nothing is going to stop your hair from thinning out or even falling out in your forties. That genetic hair-loss code has been permanently written inside of you. What that DNA does is make some of the things that are true of your father become genetically true about you.

John writes that when we receive God's covenant of love and become His children, His seed is implanted within us. When we become a new creation in Christ, the self-replicating material of the Holy Spirit transfers a holiness code in our new selves, and some of the holiness of God is spiritually and permanently written within us. When this happens, qualities that are true about God begin to manifest themselves in us.

According to John, one of the spiritually genetic manifestations of God's seed (i.e. *sperma*) being in us is our inability to stay in sin. Even though a real child of God can become guilty of committing sin, no real child of God can continue to comfortably live in sin. This is one of the benefits of God's seed being in us. We reflect the nature of His holiness with our inability to remain comfortably in sin.

His self-replicating material helps us to reflect some of His essence by motivating our constant effort to avoid sin.

But there's another spiritual manifestation of being God's child. Not only does the self-replicating material of the Holy Ghost transfer a holiness code to all of God's children, but it also transfers a code of love to every one of His real children. So not only does every child of God reflect the essence of the Father's holiness, we're also supposed to spiritually reflect the essence of the Father's love. This love should be reflected in the relationship we have not only with Him, but also with ourselves and the people around us.

When we fail to allow this to naturally take place with us and our existential relationships, however, we become guilty of mismanaging the very character of God's love, which should be a relevant component in all of our relationships. No matter if they are permanent relationships that last forever, temporary relationships that last for a season, or brief relationships that only last a moment or two, every one of our human-to-human relationships should be characterized by the reflection of God's love.

But not only do we fail to reflect the essence of His love as His children when we don't make the choice to commit to the best interests of God and others, as we practice looking after the best interests of ourselves, we also fail to reflect the essence of God's love when we turn it into something that others have to earn, or they have to become worthy to receive from us. This is a major failure based on the simple fact that God's love isn't best demonstrated when it's shared with people who deserve it. Instead, God's love is best displayed when it's shared with the undeserving, with those who are extremely unworthy of it, and with those who are frequently passed over during the very moments they need God's love the most.

But then there's a third way we mismanage our responsibility as God's children to reflect the love of the Father. It occurs when we choose to only share love exclusively with the people who reciprocate it back to us. This undoubtedly is an area that probably all of us need to re-evaluate the most. If I were to ask you to name the people you love, I'm sure you wouldn't name any of the people you don't like, because it's natural to only share your love with the people who willingly share theirs with you. As a matter of fact, these are the people who receive our love the most—the ones who reflect it back to us.

When we love like this, we think we're pleasing God. We actually believe we are satisfying the Christian requirement to love others when we love in this manner. But the truth is, when we have conditioned our love to function like this, it is failing severely to reflect the essence of the love of God. Why? Because God's love is not based on reciprocity.

God's love doesn't operate like a trade agreement. It doesn't come with conditions or established expectations. As a matter of fact, anything based on expectations, trade-off agreements, reciprocity, and equal exchange fundamentally can't be genuine love. Such conditional terms, whether expressed or unexpressed, don't come anywhere close to the expression of love in its purest form, which is unconditional. It has everything to do with you, and absolutely nothing to do with the other person.

Friends, it's critical that you understand this. Love chooses to commit to another person and their best interests in life, period—no ifs, ands, or buts about it. Expectations, trade-offs, reciprocity, conditions, and equal beneficiary arrangements are non-factors. The only real factor is your capability to choose, as well as your capacity to commit to their best interests.

You are not responsible for having a loving relationship with everybody, because some people won't allow space for you to have a loving relationship with them. What you are still responsible for is loving them with God's kind of love. You don't need them to love you in order for you to love them. All you need is your capacity to choose to commit to their best interests in life.

The reason it's so important for you to understand this is because God holds us responsible for loving everybody—even the people who not only fail to reciprocate it back to us, but also those who go so far as to hate us. The Bible refers to such people as our enemies.

Do you know who your enemies are? I've found that most people have no idea. As a result, they have labeled people as enemies who really aren't. Let me help you identify your real enemies. An enemy is the exact opposite of a neighbor. Remember, Jesus made us redefine the term when the religious leader asked him who his neighbor was. A true neighbor is someone who shares his or her love with anyone who needs it. It's a person who will choose to commit to another person's best interests in life when he or she is in the position to do so.

An enemy is the complete opposite—a person who hates you. And like love, hate is equally *not* a feeling, even though we erroneously think it is. Hate is as much a manifested choice as love is. When an enemy hates you, it means that he or she is a person who willfully neglects to choose to commit to you and your best interests in life. Not only that, they will also do all they can to hinder you and get in the way of anything in your best interests from happening for you. That's a real enemy.

The people who are jealous of you because you have more than they do are not your enemies. They're just dealing with personal insecurity that your own security makes them even more insecure about. Such people are just jealous of you. But this alone doesn't make them your enemies, though it can be a gateway for them to become your enemies.

Moreover, the people who always talk about you and your personal business are not your enemies. They just haven't built a meaningful life for themselves to keep themselves occupied. So they talk about you because doing so adds a sense of relevancy to their own lives. They need to talk about you because their own lives are uninteresting. Yet they aren't your enemies.

The people around you who can't celebrate with you because they wanted the recognition you got aren't your enemies either. They're just envious of you. They just wanted what you happened to receive. Their attitude towards you simply indicates that they don't have the emotional maturity to celebrate with you about something they wanted for themselves. But such immaturity doesn't make them your enemies.

So, everybody you believe is your enemy really isn't. Though they are jealous, envious, gossipy, and emotionally immature, they haven't devoted themselves to rejecting or fighting against any interests that may be best for you. They haven't devoted themselves to working against anything beneficial for you. They're just jealous of you, or they just don't like your personality. Maybe they just don't know how to deal with your success because it makes them feel so unaccomplished. But this doesn't make them your enemies.

No, your enemies are the people who literally hate you. They are the ones committed to rejecting everything in your best interests, and dedicated to fighting against anything beneficial for you. An enemy is an adversary, and our chief adversary is Satan.

Satan is committed to rejecting what's best for us. He is sold out to fighting against anything advantageous for us. Along with him, there are people in your life who have devoted themselves to hating you. They have committed to never being a part of anything serving your best interests, and they will fight either openly or privately against everything that may possibly benefit you. That's who your true enemies are.

But even when it comes to people like these as God's children, we are held accountable by Him for loving them. Despite our inability to have a loving relationship with them, we still must love them. What is true of the Father still must be true of us, even when it comes to our enemies.

Jesus said, "You have heard it said to love your neighbor and hate your enemy." That is the natural tendency of the heart of man. Man naturally embraces what embraces him, despises what/who despises him, and rejects whatever or whoever rejects him. There is nothing natural about loving what hates you. Yet Jesus commands us to not do the natural thing, but rather to act in a way that is greatly unnatural. He commands us to love our enemies.

This command requires us to be spiritual. You can't love your enemies in your own flesh. You have to be spiritual to love those who hate you and commit to the best for others who want the worst for you! To accomplish that, you have to be a child of God. In other words, God's seed has to be within you. God's self-replicating material has to have transported the genetic code of His love within you.

Only God has the right genetics to love those who are His enemies. Romans 5 teaches us that while we were God's enemies, Christ demonstrated His love for us by dying on the cross for our sake. We are taught that God loved us while we were still His enemies.

But not only that, this verse teaches that God allows His sun to shine on the just and unjust, as well as His rain to fall on the evil and the good. That is, there's a genetic part of the character of God that has the capacity to love and commit to the very people who hate Him and work against Him. If we are His children, and have His seed in us, we are expected to allow that genetic part of our Father's love to manifest itself in us. We are expected to not only love God, ourselves, and our neighbors, but our enemies as well. As His children, His seed gives us the capacity to do so.

When you're God's child, what is true of Him ought to be true of you too. If your Father can be kind to the ungrateful and the evil people, that self-replicating material ought to be in you as well. But if the capacity to love your enemies isn't in you, then according to the Word, you may be in God's church, but you're not one of His children. God shares His love DNA with all of His children! If you claim to be His child, but there is no resemblance of God in you when it comes to loving your enemies, the Bible says your father is the Devil.

At any rate, Jesus commands us as God's children to practice loving our enemies. Although they clearly reject us and fight against what's best for us, the Savior tells us that we're still responsible for choosing to commit to what's best for them. Christ demands that we love them.

Jesus tells us to love our enemies, do good to them, bless them, and pray for them. We should treat them completely different from the way they treat us. When they choose to commit to our worst interests, we must continue to choose to commit to their best. This is the mark of true child of God.

When they curse us and speak all manner of ill-will over us, we should speak nothing but extreme favor and goodwill over them. When they insult us and falsely accuse us, we should use our relationship with God to pray—not *about* them, but *for* them. We should ask God to move in a favorable way on their behalf.

Why does Jesus ask us to do this? The Scripture makes it clear. We are directed to do this because we get no credit from God for reciprocal love. Reciprocal love is a natural love, and we don't get credit for loving in an emotionally natural way. You don't need God in order to love somebody who loves you back. According to Jesus, even sinners do that. People who don't even believe in God do that every day. It's natural. But God hasn't called us as His children to love people naturally, but spiritually. There are no rewards for loving people in return for them loving you. God rewards those who demonstrate the ability to love the way He loves, which includes loving your enemies.

When you can treat people the way you want to be treated and never base the way you treat them by the way they treat you, there's a reward for that. When you choose to do good things for people with no expectations of them doing good back to you in order for you to continue doing good to them, there's a reward for that. When you can love the very people who fight against you, and who have absolutely no love for you, there's a reward for that. These are rewards that Jesus wants us to have and those that you should want for yourself. They can only come into your life when your love genetically represent the way He loves. Don't miss out on your rewards! Don't forfeit all God has for you because you keep allowing your feelings to get in the way of your duty to love on a different frequency, a spiritual frequency.

Final Thought

Some time ago, I was reading the historical information concerning Queen Sheba's interaction with King Solomon in I Kings 10. The Queen is said to have heard about the great wisdom of Solomon, and wanted to witness it for herself. The text tells us that Queen Sheba came to prove his wisdom with 'hard questions.' Though the Bible doesn't detail the many difficult questions presented to the King, other historical sources give great insight as to what some of her hard questions and difficult riddles.

One particular question that was presented to the King by Queen Sheba was, "what is the ugliest thing in the world, and what is the most beautiful? What is the most certain, and what is the most uncertain?" The answer that he gave was, "The ugliest thing is the faithful turning unfaithful; the most beautiful is the repentant sinner. The most certain is death; the most uncertain, one's share in the World to Come." I thought this was an interesting question that paired two sets of anti-thetical ideas: ugliest to most beautiful, and most certain to most uncertain. So, I decided to pose this same question to my wife. When I asked her, she asked for time to process it before she answered, and she left the room. However, my 6 year old son, Harrison, was in the room with me when I posed the question. Shortly after Precious left the room, clearly haven taken time to quietly process the question himself, he blurted out to me, "Dada, I know what the most beautiful thing in the world is!" I responded to him, "oh yeah? What is it son?" He answered with all sureness & great confidence — "love!"

I was so shocked! His response warmed my heart like a fire-place in the midst of a cold winter night. Though his answer was not the answer given by the wisest man to have ever walked the face of the earth (not including Jesus Christ), I was so proud to know that my 6-year old son was present enough in this often mean and cruel world to understand that there is nothing more beautiful in life than the power of love.

With this in mind, I would encourage you to embrace the power of love. To adopt it as to being the most beautiful thing not only in life, but in your life! I want you to relish this beauty, allow your life to be revived by this beauty, and delight in all the endless possibilities it can bring to you. If you want to truly have a beautiful life, you must grasp this profound revelation of love, and you must personally do the work that it takes to start living like you now know love like you have never known it before!

.

www.ingramcontent.com/pod-product-compliance
Lightning Source LLC
Chambersburg PA
CBHW060411090426
42734CB00011B/2287